# An A to Devon D

The origins of words have always fascinated me. Every item or action has to have a word or phrase to convey a message and many of the words in Devon dialect, or 'mouthspaich', are more emotive and imaginative than their 'English' equivalents. Many words evolved from a past lifestyle spent much 'closer to nature'. The language is sometimes as 'earthy' as the people themselves. A good (or is it bad?) example is 'backdoor trots', a delightful term which, if you can't work it out, is in the list.

One has only to drive through winding, muddy, high-hedged lanes past distinctly 'aromatic' farmyards to appreciate the remoteness of many parts of this large county of Devon. In the past, the people who populated these places rarely went anywhere and most had little contact with the 'outside world', so their language (and culture) was virtually unchallenged. 'Glorious Devon' is a tapestry of lush green countryside and many of the words listed here are part of that landscape.

R. N. Worth wrote in 1907:*'It was not merely in the spirit of enthusiasm that Charles Kingsley, himself by accident of birth a Devonshire man, exclaimed 'Glorious West-Country! you must not despise their accent, for it is the remains of a nobler and purer dialect than our own.' Devonshire speech ... is 'the true classic English of Alfred's time, or, as it is called, the Anglo-Saxon, is the groundwork upon which our modern English has been built up ..."*

If you are a 'furriner' (foreigner) to Devon you may recognise similar words from your own regional dialect. It therefore cannot be claimed that all the words listed here are peculiar to Devon. It is also true that not all of them would feature in the vocabulary spoken by true Devonians.

There are certain words which have been given alternative meanings by country folk. A 'chatterbox' may be a talkative person to you but to some rural dwellers it is, because of its characteristics, also a magpie.

As will be seen by the dictionary the 'z' often equates to an 's', as does 'f' become 'v', at the front of a word. The spelling of some of these dialect words is open to debate; they were meant to be said rather than written, so the way they have been recorded here is not 'gospel'. Many have small variations around the county, so if the version listed here isn't quite the one you know don't worry about it. It's really more to do with phonetics than spelling, as you will 'zee' for yourself 'zoon' enough! Many dialect words are only ordinary words but when written down in the way that they are said look like new words. Ideally dialect should only be spoken and not written. Exponents and entertainers like Tony Beard, alias 'the Widecombe Wag', and Ashburton's John Germon have certainly done their bit to keep the spoken word alive.

Many, though, have written dialect stories: William Weekes, Clement Marten and the legendary Jan Stewer (A. J. Coles, pictured opposite), to name but three. G. A. Cooke's *The County of Devon*, circa 1810, Sarah Hewitt's *The Peasant Speech of Devon*, published in 1892, and G. P. R. Pulman's *Rhymes and 'Skits'* (1871) were all compiled at a time when the use of dialect was more evident. Many others have since formed word lists. The most comprehensive collection of words was collated by Murray Laver, recorder of dialect for the Devonshire Association. Three volumes are housed at Exeter's Westcountry Studies Library and a perusal makes for fascinating reading. This little book only features a relatively small number of words, collected from a wide variety of sources.

As dialect words or expressions can be amusing I hope you will enjoy this selection, which has been arranged in an A to Z layout for easy reference. I sincerely hope you *'ave fun m' dears and make zertin sure 'e spakes prapper Deb'n the next time uz zees 'e!*

# A

**abroad** – broken to bits, split open, undone
**ace** – yes
**ackmal** – a mouth ulcer or a wren
**addle-aid** – a fool
**addle-brain** – same again!
**addled/addle-aided** – backward or confused
**addle-pit** – a cesspit
**agasted** – terrified, frightened witless
**age-traw** – a drainage ditch
**agon** – ago
**ahind** – behind
**aigs** – eggs
**ainter** – enter
**airish** – windy, often suggesting cold as well
**airy-mouse** – a bat
**aivet** – a newt
**aizy** – easy
**aizy-cheer** – an easy chair
**a-jee** – bent, buckled or crooked
**akket** – the black-headed gull
**alabash** – boiling
**alkitotle** – a silly elf
**aller** – an alder
**aller-bed** – the wet place where the water-loving alders grow
**allerbury** – an alder wood
**allern** – made from the wood of alders
**allernbatch** – an old sore
**alley** – aisle of church
**all of a diz** – bamboozled
**all of a quirk** – restless or fidgety
**all to wance** – suddenly
**all up the orchard** – involved in some unpleasant, unavoidable circumstance
**'alse** – hazel
**'alsen stick** – a dowser's hazel prong/divining rod
**American robin** – a redwing
**ammil** – derives from enamel; a glistening coating of ice covering all forms of flora and found more in northern climes, where it is known as 'the ammel'
**ammit** – lunch
**'amper** – blotchy-skin
**ancient** – a very old person
**angle-bow** – a springle for catching birds
**angle-dug or angle-twitch** – an earthworm used as fishing bait
**ankercher** – handkerchief
**Anthony pig** – the runt of the litter
**antzister** – an ancestor
**an'yels** – angels
**anzum** – handsome, a fine fellow or a good outcome
**apple-bird** – a chaffinch
**apple-blooth** – apple blossom
**appledrane** – a wasp
**applegalley** – hopscotch
**apple-thrish** – mistle-thrush
**apse or apsen** – fasten
**apurt** – sullen, silent
**arrish** – a field of stubble
**arse-auver-tap** – head over heels
**arsy-versy** – upside down
**arter** – after
**arter-awl** – after all
**arter-noon** – afternoon
**ash-cat** – a feline friend who lives and lies by the fire
**aslat** – cracked
**assiniate** – assassinate
**astrout** – stretched or taut
**athist** – thirsty
**athurt** – crosswise
**ausney** – to anticipate bad news
**aveard** – afraid
**avenin** – 'evening!', a greeting
**avire** – on fire
**avore** – before
**avroar** – frozen or frosty
**awbo or awpel** – an apple
**aw! dally-buttons!** – a joyful exclamation
**awl** – a hole
**awn** – oven
**ays** – yes
**azides** – besides

# B

**babbing titter** – a pied wagtail
**backalong** – previously, in the past
**backdoor trots** – diarrhoea
**backledge** – rear premises
**backlet** – backyard or rear courtyard
**back'ouse** – scullery
**backsivore** – back to front
**back-stick** – log at back of open-hearthed fire
**back-sun** – property where the sun only shines on the rear
**bacon 'aid** – a dim wit
**bacon 'aiters** – cockroaches
**bacon ore** – barytes mined in Teign valley
**bad-a-bed** – bedridden by illness
**bad blid** – bad blood or ill-feeling towards someone or something
**bad place** – hell

**bade** – bed
**baggabone** – a tramp or vagrant
**baggage** – term of endearment for a young girl
**baggage** – derogatory term for an older girl
**baggerin'** – annoying or greatly irritating
**bailing** – hatching out or creating a hole in an egg for an imminent birth
**baily or bealy** – a bailiff, so watch out!
**baint** – it isn't
**baissle** – to make dirty
**bait** – bad temper
**bait** – to feed a fire
**bait or bate** – food or tucker
**baked** – surprised
**balderation** – a disturbance
**ball** – a rounded hill, common on Southern Dartmoor, eg Corringdon Ball
**ball** – to track animals by their footprints
**ball** – to thrash
**ballard** – a ram which has been castrated
**ball-bagger** – a noisy person
**ballet** – a slow song or ballad
**ballidraunt** – an imbecile
**ballirag or ballyrag** – to reprimand, chastise, scold or abuse
**Banbury talk** – gobbledigook
**bander** – a boundary
**banger** – something big
**banging-gert** – very big
**bankie** – a willow warbler
**bannee** – to rudely contradict someone
**banstickle** – stickleback
**banyan** – a noisy uproar or assembly
**banyan days** – when food or money is short
**bar-duck** – shelduck
**bare-ridged ridin'** – riding bare-back
**barker** – a grindstone
**barley-burd** – a seagull
**barley-drake** – a corncrake
**barley-gout** – shingles (illness)
**barley-ile** – the beard of ripe barley
**barm** – yeast
**barnacles** – spectacles
**barn-screecher** – a barn owl
**Barnstaple oven** – one lined with clay
**baron-bill** – a guillemot
**barrel** – two bushels of lime (16 gallons)
**barricoes** – sturdy fences
**barrow-pig** – a gelt pig
**barthless** – homeless
**basky-burd** – a yellow bunting
**bate** – to quarrel
**bate, batyn, baty** – to decrease

**bateborough** – couch grass or other weeds
**battel** – to fertilise
**battin'** – netting birds by night
**bautch** – an error or mistake
**bawked-up** – shut off from sight, concealed
**bay-spittal** – honey
**be** – am
**beagle** – an awkward cuss
**beaver** – lunch-time
**bed-ale** – ale to celebrate the arrival of a new baby or the homecoming of newly-weds
**bedlier** – an invalid or a lazy lie-a-bed
**beedle-heyde** – the bullhead or 'miller's thumb', a small freshwater fish
**bees' tongues** – foxgloves
**beget** – to forget
**begorsey** – a term of exclamation, 'By God!'
**begurge or begridge** – begrudge
**belk** – to belch
**beller** – to bawl
**bell-harm** – the colic
**bellises/billises** – bellows
**bellisher** – an exhausting job
**bell-jessy** – a top hat
**bell-rose** – daffodil
**belly-timber** – food or nourishment
**bescumber** – to dirty
**bettermost** – of a higher social class
**betty** – to potter about
**between the lights** – twilight
**between two worlds** – in a fainting state
**bevower** – before
**beznez** – business
**bezooks** – going berserk/really angry
**bibble** – to drink often
**bibble-bugs** – woodlice
**bicker** – to move slowly along a valley
**bickety-rug** – a most awkward child
**bide** – await
**bides** – remains
**bield** – a sheepfold
**big-about** – a strapping physique
**bigetty** – arrogant
**biggin** – a coffee-pot
**billy-buttons** – woodlice (again!)
**bimbye** – by-and-by
**bird's eye** – speedwell or red campion or any number of plants
**biscake** – biscuit
**bissle** – dirty, beastly
**bit-ago** – a short time since
**bitagone** – lately
**bitterweed** – an ill-tempered person

**bivver** – to quivver with fear or shake with cold
**bizzens** – business
**black aid** – tadpole
**black army** – fleas
**black as up Lover** – as suitably dark as Lovers' Lane needs to be!
**blackdrish** – blackbird
**black-looking** – cross, frowning, ill-tempered
**black-pot** – pudding made of pig's blood, groats etc
**black-psalm** – the doleful cry of a child
**blacks** – clothes worn during mourning
**blacktail** – stoat
**bladder** – to talk incessantly
**bladders** – blisters
**blaked-away** – cried till breathless
**blamed** – a polite swear
**blare** – shout loudly at or scold
**bliddy** – bloody
**bliddy warriors/bloody war'yers** – wallflowers
**blind man's holiday** – when it's too dark to carry on working
**bline-mobbed** – blindfolded
**blinket** – the appearance of the sky just before a major snowfall
**blinks** – flames
**blooth** – bloom/blossom
**blue-ass flies** – blow flies or bluebottles
**blue bonnet** – a blue tit
**blue hawk** – a merlin
**blunk** – spark
**bobbery** – a major bust-up or uproar
**bobbing** – fishing for eels
**bobbing Joan** – a sprightly young maiden
**bobs-a-dying** – a big row
**bone** – a tooth
**boneshave** – sciatica
**boodies** – beauties (a term of endearment when preceded with 'my')
**bosky** – slightly drunk
**botch** – a blotchy complexion/skin eruption
**bother** – deafen
**bottle-washer** – a pied wagtail
**Bovey or Buvvy** – a plain bun eaten with jam and cream
**bow** – a bodily joint
**bowled** – boiled
**boy-chap** – a male teenager or adolescent
**brad or brod** – a thick stick
**Bradbury tigers** – Dartmoor foxes
**braget-cat** – a grey tabby
**bragety** – mottled
**brand-bete** – to kindle or rekindle a fire

**brandis** – a four-legged stand, like a trivet but bigger
**brangle** – to quarrel
**braund** – a log of fire-wood
**brave** – excellent of its type
**brawk** – broken or out of money
**brawn** – a massive yuletide log which was burned during the twelve days of Christmas
**brekzis** – breakfast
**brewer** – heather
**brimbles** – brambles
**brimbly** – having lots of brambles
**briss** – dust
**brit** – to dent
**britivul** – beautiful
**brocky** – a tramp
**broodle** – to brood
**brookin'** – drying
**broozle-up** – waking up, wising up
**brown hawk** – kestrel or the rusty-back fern
**brownkittee** – bronchitis
**browsy** – red-faced or robust
**brunchen** – virgin soil tilled for the first time
**buckle** – a struggle
**buckle-tu** – to work with a will
**bud-burd** – bullfinch
**buddle** – to get drunk
**bud-tit** – great tit
**buffle-'aided** – stupid
**bug-blind** – whitewash
**bulderin' clouds** – storm clouds
**buldery** – thundery
**bulkee** – a belch, what relief!
**bullbagger/bull-beggar** – a scarecrow
**bull's neck** – a grudge
**bull's noon** – an indefinite period
**bull walloper** – cattle trader
**bum** – a bailiff
**bumbledore** – bumblebee
**bumbledory** – cockchafer
**bummings an' scrapings** – ordinary folk
**bumscuddy** – a tight, revealing garment, a mini-skirt
**bungy/busky** – short, stunted, stout
**bunk** – to drop
**bunting** – butting
**hup** – a nuisance
**hurdge** – a bridge
**burgin** – a bargain
**burkee** – to cough
**burly-vace** – pimply face or poor complexion
**buskins** – short leggings
**busky-eyed** – drunk

**butcher-burd** – a buzzard
**butt** – a beehive
**butter and barley weather** – mild, wet and muggy weather
**button-hearted** – ruthless, tough, unyielding
**button-short** – half-witted
**butt-woman** – a female verger or sextoness
**buzzard** – a butterfly or moth
**buzzymilk** – the first milk after calving
**by-Gar!** – by God!

## C

**cab-a-dab** – a merry, mirth-making person
**cabbage** – to purloin
**cabbage-raced** – inexperienced
**cabbical** – excellent
**cack** – left-handed
**cacky** – a wren
**caddick** – a thick stick
**caddling** – idling or loafing about
**caddy-ball** – tennis ball
**cagg-mag** – bad meat
**cannibal** – a sparrow hawk
**caper** – bit of a rum do, a right old carry-on
**carpet-slipper courting** – couples going out together from the same area
**cat ice** – a thin coating of ice on a lake, which will bear a cat and little else
**cat-lap** – tea
**cat o' nine tails** – hazel catkins
**cauchy** – muddy, sticky
**cautch** – mess
**cautcheries** – medicines
**cawed** – diseased
**cess** – luck or happiness
**chaffer** – a chaffinch
**chaize** – cheese
**cham** – chew
**cham auver** – chew or mull over
**chance-child** – bastard
**changeling** – a child believed to have been swapped by fairies. The exchanged offspring is often either ugly or stupid or both
**chank/chawk** – jackdaw
**chap-full** – full to the top
**charmer** – a white witch
**chatterbox** – a magpie
**chaynee-eyed** – squinting
**cheal or cheel** – baby or child
**cheat the crows** – to recover from a life-threatening illness
**cheerybangs** – charabancs
**cheese-bugs** – woodlice (popular aren't they?)

**Cherry-fair** – once numerous and held on Sundays, the evenings were reserved for lovers to ramble or romantically roam in orchards or large country gardens
**cherry-gog** – the cherry stone
**chestlecrumbs** – dormice
**chets** – kittens
**chibbles** – spring onions
**Chick-Chack Day** – Oak Apple Day (29 May)
**chicket** – cheerful
**chicksy-pixie** – of a substandard quality
**chilbladders** – chilblains
**chillern** – children
**chim-cham** – idle banter, gossip, tittle-tattle
**chimie-shirt** – vest
**chimley** – chimney
**chink** – a chaffinch
**chip** – to share a joke, how appropriate!
**chitch-hatch** – churchyard gate
**chitlins/chittlins** – intestines
**chockling** – cackling
**chollers** – cheeks (facial ones!)
**chonchabells/chonchables** – icicles
**chorer** – a charlady
**chow** – to nag
**chowder** – female fish seller
**chubbleheaded** – stupid
**chucked** – choked
**chuckvul** – drunk, again!
**Chudleys/Chudleighs** – plain buns eaten with jam and cream
**chuff** – ill-tempered
**chun** – a bad woman
**chunner** – to argue
**chur** – fast-moving
**clabby** – sticky and sweet
**clapper** – tongue
**clapper-claw** – to reprimand
**clarent** – partly grown
**clatting** – fishing for eels using worms strung on worsted and attached to the end of a pole, apparently best done by night
**claws** – clothes
**cleachy** – luke-warm
**cleck- or click-ma-doodle** – item which has seen better days
**clecky** – feeble
**cledgee** – sticky
**click-ma-toad** – any kind of machinery
**cliff hawk** – peregrine falcon
**clint** – a deed of oneupmanship; or to bend the point of a nail and also to confirm
**clipper** – a knock on the head

**clit** – heavy
**clitched-hold** – caught
**Clitch Fair** – a fair held at Dodbrooke, Kingsbridge, where buns were extracted, by mouth, from a vat of treacle
**clitchy** – tacky
**clitty** – close
**cloam/clome** – earthenware/glazed china
**cloamin' cat** – a greedy person
**cloamy** – clayey
**clockee** – a hen's cackle
**clod pole** – a rustic or yokel
**clop** – to limp or walk with difficulty
**close-visted** – tight or mean
**Clovelly woodcock** – a herring
**clowted craime** – clotted cream
**club** – stout
**clunk** – to swallow
**clunker/clunter** – a swallow
**cockleert** – dawn
**cock tiddly** – a wren
**cod** – a pheasant
**coddy-noddy** – a young seagull
**codwall** – a woodpecker
**college** – houses at the back of others and approached by a passage or 'drang'!
**Collop Monday** – day before Shrove Tuesday
**colly** – a blackbird
**comical** – ill-tempered
**condiddle** – to waste, to convey away secretly
**condudle** – conceit
**conjuror** – a male witch or warlock
**conkables/conkerbills** – icicles
**coochy-paw** – clumsy chap
**copper-clouts** – leggings
**corrosy** – a grudge, bad feeling
**counterfeit** – a hermit crab
**courtledge** – small backyard of a house
**cow-comforts** – stone pillars erected on Dartmoor for cattle so that they can rub themselves
**cowflop** – a foxglove
**crabbity** – cantankerous or peevish
**cradid** – acidy
**crams** – nonsense
**crap** – crop
**creedle** – to crawl
**cribble-fly** – dragonfly
**cricket** – a three-legged stool
**crilly** – curly
**crimbs** – crumbs
**crim-up** – shrivel-up
**crimminy!** – an expletive of pure surprise
**cring-crankum** – not straight

**crinkle-crankle** – zig-zag or twisted
**crinkum-crankums** – fidgets
**crinnicks** – dead wood
**crint** – to groan, grunt or complain
**cripple** – a snake or lizard
**chrisemore** – unbaptised child
**croak** – to die
**crocky-stew** – potato stew
**crooked words** – swearing
**crope** – to strangle
**crowd** – a fiddle or violin
**crowder** – a fiddler
**crowdy pies** – apple dumplings or a pie made from mutton chops, onions and apples
**crown** – to hold an inquest
**crownation** – a coronation
**crowner** – a coroner
**crub** – a trough
**cruel-quiet** – silent
**crummit** – edible items eaten between meals
**cubby-down** – a little girl
**cuddie/cuddley** – a wren
**cuddie-bum** – having a short tail
**cuff** – light and trivial conversation
**cuff it auver** – argue the toss
**culver** – wood pigeon or dove
**culver house** – a dovecot
**cunnin'** – hard to find or root out
**curly-handle** – a double-barrelled name
**Cursemas** – Christmas
**cussen** – to train or teach
**Cutty Dyer** – evil water sprite from Ashburton

# D

**daberdash** – to spoil
**dabfinch** – chaffinch
**Daddy** – the Devil
**daffadowndillies** – daffodils
**daggle** – to run like a youngster
**dallylaw** – a spoilt child
**dander-up** – to become incensed
**dandy-go-risset** – rusty brown
**dang-my-old-wig** – a swearing term
**dap** – slap
**dapper** – best behaviour
**daps** – a strong likeness
**Dartmoor stables** – mires
**dashed** – a swear
**dashels** – thistles
**dashful** – shy
**dashus** – audacious
**datchin or daychin** – thatching
**daun 'ee?** – don't you?
**daw-bake** – a slow-witted person

**dawbwoys** – dough-dumplings
**dawcock** – a silly fellow
**daylights** – eyes
**dead waste** – a graveyard
**Debbenshure** – Devonshire
**Debbenshure Moile** – a 'Devonshire Mile' ie about 2 miles!
**Deb'm/De'm** – Devon
**deef** – rotten
**deeve** – (pardon?) deaf!
**Devil's blossom** – hemlock
**Devil's coach-hoss** – a beetle commonly found in N. Devon
**Devil's darning needles** – dragonflies
**Devil's door** – door on north side of a church
**Dewar** – the Devil, again
**dew snail** – slug
**dibbet** – a small amount
**dibby** – small
**dibs** – money
**diddlecombe** – half mad, sorely vexed
**dimmet** – getting dark, dusk
**dimpsey** – still getting dark!
**dinder** – thunder
**dishwasher** – the wagtail
**ditties or ditty-guys** – gipsies
**dizzy-belled** – undressed
**docity** – having a quick-witted nature
**doil** – to prattle incoherently
**dollican** – a ship's toilet
**dollop** – onomatopoeia at its best!
**dolly-mop** – an idle person
**donnikin** – like the Aussie 'dunny' is a toilet at the end of a garden
**doomshaw** – a procession or circus
**dot** – a small person
**dough-bake** – a soft-hearted but stupid fellow
**douse** – dust
**Dowel** – the Devil, again, again!
**dowlish** – devilish
**downdacious** – audacious
**down-under** – the countryside in the shadow of upland Dartmoor
**doxy-maid** – a flirt
**drabbitted** – bad-tempered
**drade** – drawn or thrown
**drang/drangway** – back alley or passageway
**draysh** – thrash
**drayzack** – a person who speaks in a lazy manner
**dreckly** – soon
**dree** – three
**dree chairs!** – three cheers!

**drench** – to pour medicine down an animal's throat
**dreng** – to crowd
**drest-all** – a scarecrow
**drexil or drishall** – threshold
**dring** – to crowd, to push
**droo** – through
**drot** – throat
**drow** – to dry
**drubbit!** – damn!
**drumble or drummel drane** – bumblebee
**dry drizzle** – fine rain (if there is such a thing!)
**dubbed** – blunt
**duberous** – dubious
**duds** – clothes
**dug** – dog
**dugged** – muddy
**duggletailed** – skirts coverd with mud
**dumducketty** – drab, dull, dreary or all three!
**dummon** – a woman
**dunch** – deaf
**dungcart** – self-explanatory
**dunnaw** – don't know (that's what it means!)
**durns** – doorposts
**dwalee** – to talk inconsistently

# E

**'e** – it, him, her, she or he!
**eagle** – a buzzard
**eddikayshun** – education
**ees** – yes
**eezel** – himself
**ee** – him or you
**elong** – slanted
**elsh** – new
**emmet** – an ant
**erbons** – ribbons
**eved** – thawed
**every whips 'n a while** – every so often
**ezackally-zo** – just so
**ezel-pipe** – throat

# F

**facket 'ood** – brushwood
**faddy** – restless or fidgety
**faintified** – feeling dizzy
**fair to middlin'** – average, not bad, so-so
**fair to poor** – not so wonderful!
**fairy thimbles** – foxgloves again
**fakement** – a muddle
**fandangles** – ladies' jewellery
**fanty** – ridiculous
**fantysheeny** – extremely fanciful

**fardel/fardle** – found in place names, a bundle, package or load
**Farewell Summer** – the robin
**fat-shag** – bacon
**fawny** – a finger ring
**feel fairy** – in a jovial mood or in fine health, buoyant
**fell-digger** – a rat
**fess** – smart
**fettled up** – dressed up for a night out
**fewster** – fester
**fid-fad** – waste time, idle about
**figgy-pudden** – Christmas pudding
**filly-loo** – an uproar
**fitch** – weasel, polecat or ferret
**fizz** – anger
**flammakin** – a coarse woman
**flaw** – as luck would have it a gust of wind
**flawn** – a pancake
**fleet-water** – flood water (*fleot* is an old word for river)
**flex** – an animal pelt
**flibberts or flibbits** – small bits
**flickermayte** – mixture of milk and flour
**flickets** – blushes
**flid** – a flood
**flim-flam** – malicious or wilful gossip
**flink** – a quick or sudden movement/to sprinkle
**flittereens** – small pieces
**flittermouse** – a bat, animal type!
**floor** – flat meadow beside a river
**floppy-doc** – foxglove again
**flother** – boastful banter
**flower-nat** – a flower bed
**flummix** – to frighten
**flushy-faiver** – the flu
**fore-right** – straightforward
**forker** – a swallow (possibly because of its forked tail)
**franager** – to thieve or steal
**frappy** – short-tempered
**frawzy** – a treat, a tasty tit-bit, a dainty feast
**Frenchnits** – walnuts
**fricker** – a pest
**frickety** – heavy, sodden
**fricky** – restless
**fries** – not chips but fried lambs' testicles, ugh!
**frinder** – to excite
**frisk** – a light shower of rain
**frisky rain** – very fine drizzle
**froward** – a promontory or headland, there is Froward Point near Brixham
**fuddler** – a drunkard

**fuddly** – drunk
**fustilugs** – big-boned, sloppily dressed woman!
**fustled-up** – wrapped-up
**fuzz-pig** – hedgehog

# G

**gabbee** – incessant banter
**gabbin** – talking
**gaddle** – weak
**gage** – a full set of dentures
**galdiment** – a scare or fright
**gallases** – gibbet or gallows
**gallied** – frightened
**gallitraps** – any mysterious signs or circles; ugly ornaments; or poorly-made tools or devices
**gallivantin** – gadding about, flirting
**gally** – to scare
**gally-bagger** – a person fond of gadding about
**gally-gawk** – a scarecrow
**gambakers** – the opposite of nimble-footed
**gammuts** – games
**gammy-handed** – a hand incapable of much movement
**gapnistering** – staring idly about
**gapper-mouth** – an imbecile
**gastable** – ill-behaved
**gaysome** – in a cheerful or merry mood
**gennel or ginnel** – a narrow passage, a 'drang'!
**gibby-lambs** – very young lambs
**giglet** – a happy-go-lucky young maiden
**giglet market** – from where maid-servants were hired
**ginged** – bewitched
**girlop** – a big lout
**gladdie** – a fool
**gladdy** – the yellowhammer
**gleanies** – guinea fowl
**glib** – to castrate
**glubby** – 'tight-arsed' or mean
**gobble-guts** – a greedy person
**God-a'mighty's cow** – ladybird
**goggle** – to down a drink swiftly
**going to the lew** – becoming bankrupt
**gommer** – an elderly lady
**goo'coos** – bluebells
**Goodger** – the devil
**gooze cap** – an idiot
**goozegogs** – gooseberries
**gor-belly** – big belly
**goyle** – deep, steep valley, common in E. Devon
**gramferlonglegs** – long-legged spiders and flies
**granfer griggs** – woodlice (they are everywhere!)

**greysidaisy** – the daffodil
**groaning-ale** – beer brewed to celebrate birth of a baby
**groaning dame** – midwife
**grockle** – a visitor to Devon
**grockle bait** – things that a visitor might buy
**groot-varm** – an arable farm
**groot rest** – soil lying fallow
**guddify** – to become extremely religious or devout
**gulchy** – fat
**gulging** – drinking greedily
**gump 'aid** – a stupid person
**gurt** – great
**gushment** – a sudden fright
**guttering** – eating greedily
**guzzle guts** – over-indulgence in 'booze'
**gwain** – going
**gwain-vore** – getting close

# H

**hacty** – lively, active
**hag-begag** – to bewitch
**haggage** – an unkempt woman
**half-a-mind** – tempted to do something
**ham-cham** – to pause for a chat
**harbourers** – those who stalk or hunt deer
**harbs** – herbs
**harrage** – a disturbance
**Harry Eight Legs** – a spider
**hatchmouthed** – coarse, vulgar in speech
**hawchee** – to eat in a noisy fashion
**hay digees** – in a buoyant mood
**hazy-dazy** – slap-happy or of a careless nature
**heckamal** – tom-tit
**hear-tell** – discovered by word of mouth
**heed-a-peep** – remaining out of sight
**heedy-peep** – a game of hide and seek
**hekkety-pound** – a game of hopscotch
**heller** – a little devil
**hellins** – roofing slates
**hemel** – frozen mist or fog
**hemparent** – cheeky
**hend** – to throw
**her** – can also be 'he' or any inanimate object! Usually used instead of 'she'
**hibbit** – a newt
**hide-nur-tide** – news
**high-by-day** – in broad daylight
**hinkling** – an inkling with an 'h'.
**historical** – hysterical
**hizy-prizy** – sharp practice, dubious dealing
**hoaks** – in playing cards the clubs
**hoddy-noddy** – drunk, giddy, or losing control

**hogminny** – a young girl of ill-repute
**holster** – a disturbance or fracas
**homalong** – homeward
**homescreech** – mistle-thrush
**hookem-snivey or hugger-mugger** – deceitful actions, underhand
**hookered** – worn-out, knackered!
**hootin' cough** – whooping cough
**hose-burd** – a scoundrel
**hot-evil** – the fever
**house-bait** – food
**house-cat** – a home-lover
**hozeburd** – a term of mild abuse
**huck-muck** – a dirty, dishevelled person
**huffilant** – an elephant
**hugger-mugger** – untidy, underhand
**hulch** – a thick slice
**hulder** – an extremely loud noise
**hulkin'** – slouching, of awkward gait
**humman** – woman
**hummer** – a monster lie or gross untruth
**hum-scritch** – a bluebottle
**hum-strum** – easy-going temperament
**hurd or hurdy** – red or reddish
**huxens** – various parts of the leg

# I

**icybells** – icicles
**idle-pin** – the doing of trifling things as an excuse for industry!
**idocity** – good sense
**iked-up** – puckered
**image** – a statue or possibly a scarecrow
**in-betwixt** – between
**innards** – intestines
**in 'ome** – indoors
**in two quiffs** – almost immediately, soon
**ippet** – a lizard
**iss-fay** – yes, certainly
**itemy** – full of tricks
**ivy-bush** – rough unkempt hair

# J

**jabberment** – idle banter or gossip
**jackie-twoad** – will-o'-the-wisp
**jack-up** – abandon or give up
**jakes** – toilets, excrement or confusion
**janders** – jaundice
**janner's day** – market day
**jewsire** – devilish
**jibber** – a lazy horse
**jibber-ugly's-fule** – a selfish person
**jibes** – an eccentrically-dressed person
**jiggered** – an oath

**jimcrack** – fragile or feeble
**jimmerack** – shoddily made goods
**jing** – to bewitch
**jis** – just
**jobber** – a livestock dealer or a carrier of wool
**jock** – to deal in buying/selling horses
**joggarty** – geography
**jollop** – medicine
**joney** – an ornament
**jonick** – genuine, honest, above board
**jouds** – rags
**journey** – a day's work for a peat-cutter, forty yards long and two turveyors wide
**jowder** – fish seller
**jower** – to grumble
**jumpsome** – restless
**junket** – curds and cream

# K

**kaddy-ball** – tennis ball
**kail-alley** – skittle alley
**kainy** – peep
**kank** – a worthless person
**kannel** – a candle
**kayning** – looking
**keat** – a buzzard
**keepness** – a mistress
**kerning** – ripening
**kerp** – to tell-off
**kerpee** – to find fault
**ketch vore** – catch up/overtake
**keyballs** – pine cones
**kib** – to repair a hedge
**kibby** – a chilblain
**kibe** – chilblain
**kick hammer** – someone who stammers
**kickshaw** – a derogatory term for an 'entertainment'; a useless ornament; or an untidy person
**kiggling** – unsafe or dangerous
**kill-devil** – an artificial minnow or a place in an exposed location
**kindiddled** – lured or enticed
**kintintid** – contented
**kirbies** – horse droppings
**kit** – a buzzard
**kitch** – catch
**kith** – relatives
**kittle** – kettle
**kitty-top** – a wren
**knackers or knockers** – mine-dwelling pixies who warn of imminent cave-ins if regularly fed
**knacking-vore** – getting on
**knacky** – dim-witted

**knaw-nort** – ignorant
**kommical** – curious
**kris-hawk** – kestrel
**Kurzmus** – 'We wish you a Merry Kurzmus!'
**kutch-pawed** – left-handed

# L

**lablolly** – a silly person
**lairy/leery** – hungry or empty
**lambfashion** – in youthful style
**lamb in salad** – relaxed
**lamiger** – a cripple
**lammiger** – lame, laid up with illness
**lantern-sweat** – wire netting
**lap-clap** – a noisy kiss
**larancy-weather** – thundery, oppressive weather
**lard-up** – tart-up
**larn** – learn
**larrapin'** – a thrashing or beating
**larry or lerry** – hill mist that rolls down into a valley bottom
**latch** – wish, fancy
**laurence** – laziness
**lay-by** – to be confined to bed
**lazy wind** – a biting, chilling wind
**lears** – pasture land
**leather-burd** – a bat
**leechway** – the path to a graveyard
**leedler** – smaller
**leery** – empty or hungry
**Lentshard Day** – Shrove Tuesday
**Lentshard Night** – first Monday in Lent
**lewment** – a shelter
**lewth** – the side out of the wind, leeward!
**lewzide** – to leeward
**libbits** – rags
**lich** – a corpse
**lich-bell** – one tolled for the dead
**lickerdish** – liquorice
**licky-brath** – leek stew or broth
**lied-by-the-wall** – 'twixt death and a funeral
**lights** – lungs
**li'l** – little
**limeash** – concrete
**linhay** – a shed with one side open
**lippity-lopping** – limping
**litter-legged** – like a drowned rat, bedraggled!
**lobber** – to eat piggishly
**lob's pound** – jail
**lobzided** – unbalanced
**long-cripple** – dragon-fly, lizard or a snake
**long dug** – greyhound
**long-tailed rabbit** – pheasant
**looby-louty** – a cry-baby

**lowster** – to work hard
**lurrapin'** – a beating

# M

**macket or maggie** – a magpie
**mackintoshes** – woodlice (what else?)
**macrobies** – creepy-crawly creatures
**maister** – master
**maiden** – a teenage girl
**main-zorry** – very sorry
**make-bates** – trouble-makers or spuddlers
**mallywallops** – a tall untidy woman
**malscral** – caterpillar
**many-hearted** – soft-hearted
**mapling** – a difficult child (aren't they all?)
**map-mouthed** – having no teeth
**mappers** – talkative boys
**mapsing** – smacking one's lips
**market-merry** – drunk!
**marrabones** – knees
**marrows** – colleagues
**master fag** – a cigar
**masts** – acorns
**matrimony** – gin & whisky; gin & rum
**maunderin'** – muttering
**mauxy** – untidy
**Maygames** – frolics
**may-jim** – between small and big
**mazed** – mad
**mazed-finch** – wagtail
**mazy-jack** – the village simpleton
**meetinger** – a Non-conformist
**men-volks** – menfolk
**mew or mewy** – seagull or cry of same, many offshore rocks called Mew Stone
**mezel** – myself
**middlin'** – reasonably good
**mimpsy-pimsy** – dainty
**miscall** – abuse
**mitchin'** – staying away or avoiding school
**mite** – a little
**mixen** – a dung heap
**mixy-go volks** – social climbers
**mizmaized** – dismayed
**mizzle** – a mist
**Modbury mud** – a potent ale brewed to celebrate the birth of a baby at Modbury, sometimes referred to as 'nappy-ale'
**mommet** – scarecrow
**moogits** – tree stumps
**mooster** – to get a move on
**mops and brooms** – drunk, again!
**mortal** – very much
**mountain tulips** – foxgloves, again

**mouthspaich** – dialect
**mucks/mux** – wet mud
**mucker** – a difficulty, a misfortune
**muffle or murfle-vaced** – freckled
**mulligrubs** – a fit of pique
**mumblin'** – talking quietly to oneself
**mumchance** – silent, moody
**mump 'aid** – a foolish person
**murchy** – mischief
**muty-hearted** – soft-hearted, sensitive
**muzcrawl** – caterpillar
**muzzle** – chin

# N

**nack** – knock
**naips** – turnips
**naish** – delicate
**namits, nammits, or nimmits** – come from the Anglo-Saxon *non-mete* meaning noon meat so this may be a second luncheon
**napper** – a farm boy
**nappercase** – the head
**narramored** – exceedingly angry
**nart or nort** – nothing
**natlins** – intestines
**nattled** – contracted, shrunk
**naw** – know
**nawd** – knew
**neighbouring** – idle gossiping
**nettle** – to offend
**niash** – delicate
**niddick** – the nape of the neck
**niffed** – offended
**nigh-handy** – nearby
**nimmits** – lunch (see 'namits')
**nimpingang** – to fester under the finger-nail
**nip-cheese** – a miser
**nissel-tripe** – the smallest of the litter
**nit** – nut
**noggin** – a quarter of a pint
**nonsical** – nonsensical
**nooze-bags** – gossips
**northering** – foolish, wild, incoherent
**not half-saved** – foolish
**nubby** – the nose
**nug** – a bunch

# O

**obfuscation** – drunkeness
**oddmedods or oogsy-wipples** – snails
**odzooks!** – for God's sake!
**ole dumman** – 'old woman' or wife
**ole apple umman** – an unmanly-like man
**ole todger** – old man

**olford** – orphan
**oliver** – young eel or elver
**olt** – hold
**onlight** – to dismount
**oozle** – whistle or 'wet your oozle', have a drink!
**ope** – passage, common on Plymouth's Barbican eg 'Basket Ope'
**opstropulus** – obstreperous
**orchits** – orchids
**ornywink** – lapwing
**ort** – something
**orts** – scraps or leftovers
**orts day** – traditionally Monday, when leftovers were used to make a cheap meal
**oss** – horse
**ossifer** – officer
**over-crap** – an excess
**overgit** – overtake
**owdacious** – brash

# P

**paiksin' about** – messing about
**paixy** – untidy, dirty
**pakey** – feeling out of sorts
**palm of the foot** – ball of the foot
**palsh** – to trudge slowly, often through soft or miry ground
**paper-skulled** – stupid
**parky or packy** – cold
**parson** – a rook or possibly a magpie
**passon** – parson
**passon's pig** – the fattest of the litter
**pauchin'** – poaching
**paunch** – to remove animals' innards or handle unnecessarily
**paver-lewdy** – a spoilt brat
**pawking** – walking leisurely
**pays** – peas
**peddle-backed** – round-shouldered
**pellum/pillum/pilm** – dust
**pexy** – pixie
**pig's looze** – a pigsty
**pilgarlic** – a person worthy of pity
**piss-a-bed** – dandelion
**pixie flax** – cotton grass
**pixie led** – lost
**plancheen** – floorboards
**platter-vooted** – flat-footed
**pluff** – not well
**plum** – warm, comfortable or soft
**pock-fridden** – pitted with the after-effects of smallpox

**pon tap** – on top
**pooch** – screw up one's face
**poorlified** – unwell
**pope** – the puffin (Lundy parrot)
**popples** – pebbles (as in Newton Poppleford)
**pote** – to kick about in bed
**pot-logic** – stupid remarks
**prake** – to wander about
**prate-apace** – talkative
**primrosen** – more than one primrose
**prinked** – dressed smartly
**prinky-dinky** – titivating
**proffer** – to avoid someone
**proud ladies** – foxgloves, yet again
**pudden-dag rawd** – no through road
**puggled** – confused
**pulk** – stagnant pond
**pun tap** – on top
**pupper** – dust
**purty** – pretty
**purty-vitty** – pretty good
**pusky** – short-winded or breathless
**pussy** – puffed, short-winded
**putt** – a mud cart
**puzzlement** – a mystery

# Q

**quaddle** – to waddle
**quane** – a queen
**quardle** – quarrel
**quarl** – to quarrel, ok?
**quarrel-picker** – a glazier
**Quarrenders** – red apples peculiar to Devon
**quat** – dead
**quelstring** – sweltering
**querking** – grunting
**quickin** – a frog
**quirkin'** – complaining
**quott** – sit down in a squatting position

# R

**rabberdasters** – rumped-up
**rabberdasters** – woodlice
**rabbert** – rabbit
**rabbert-catcher** – a buzzard
**rabbit** – an oath
**ragrowstering** – romping
**ragstone** – a stone used to sharpen utensils
**ram-cat** – a tom-cat
**randigals** – rumours, stories
**randy-voo** – an uproar or disturbance
**rantankersome** – cantankerous
**ranticomscour** – an uproar

**rasher-wagon** – a frying-pan
**ravel** – to untwist
**rayme** – to stretch
**raymes** – a painfully thin person, a skeleton
**readship** – trust, confidence
**regillations** – rules
**rezzevoy** – reservoir
**right deer** – one more than six years old
**rimlets** – remnants
**rinagate** – a gadabout
**rind** – (rhymes with sinned) ran
**rinner** – a round towel
**ripping-gert** – very large!
**ripping-up** – recalling
**rixen** – rushes
**rogues' roost** – an accumulation of rubbish
**rolly** – a crowd
**rookler** – young pig
**roomaticks** – rheumatic pains
**rory-tory** – gaudy, dressed in many colours
**rot-land** – land lying fallow
**rody-dow** – a disturbance, again!
**rowstering** – romping
**ruggling** – hard, tiresome work
**rumbustuous** – noisy
**rummage** – nonsense
**rummidge** – rubbish
**rum-taxed** – wrecked
**rumped-up** – humped
**runk** – offensive

# S

**Sally Hatch** – an overdressed woman
**sam-ope** – a half-open or half-closed door
**sappy** – weak-headed
**sass** – impertinence
**sass-box** – an impertinent person
**sassidger** – a sausage
**sawk** – a timid person
**scad** – shower of rain/passing shower
**scaddy** – showery
**scald-crame** – clotted cream
**scamble-hocks** – two left feet
**scamlin** – irregular
**scammel-vated** – clumsy
**scaramouche** – scarecrow
**scat** – shower of rain, this time a dashing one
**scawvy** – a word to describe smeared glass
**sclum** – scratch with nails
**sclum-cat** – a nasty or spiteful person
**scraling** – very small or crawling
**scrats** – little things
**scrawdle** – to crouch

**screwy** – tight, with money
**scriddick** – a remnant
**scruft-ass** – a villain
**scrumps** – small apples
**scrumpy** – farm cider (rocket fuel!)
**scummer/skummer** – muddle or mess
**seg** – to shake
**semolina** – salmonella (could be confusing!)
**sensible** – well briefed
**shab-off** – to leave ashamed
**shaky trade** – jelly
**shanty** – a noisy argument
**sheeny** – fanciful
**sherds/shords** – bits of broken pottery
**shet** – shoot
**shet-leke** – a millpond
**shettles** – five of these constitute a five-bar gate!
**shindle stones** – roofing slates
**shiners** – large slabs of slate used as field boundaries, particularly in the South Hams
**Shitzack Day** – 29 May
**shivers** – very small pieces
**shords** – broken earthenware or gaps in hedges
**shrammed** – feeling extremely cold
**sig/zig** – urine
**sight** – much more
**siss** – a big fat woman or to throw or aim
**sissa** – a fuss
**shriddicks** – small pieces, virtually worthless
**shugg** – shy
**skail-alley** – skittle alley
**skammel** – to walk badly
**skat** – a slap or to fling
**skeiner** – rascal or villain
**skiddy-bum** – a person of small stature
**skiffy rain** – light drizzle
**skimmished** – drunk
**skither** – sprinkle
**skitters** – diarrhoea
**skittery** – slippery
**skrent** – to burn or singe
**skritch** – screech
**skritch owl** – tawny owl
**skun** – to browbeat
**slamicking/slommickin'** – untidy, slovenly
**slew** – ostentatious show
**slicket** – a small slice of cake
**slockster** – a small-time thief
**slodge** – sledgehammer
**sloke** – entice
**slope** – to rot
**slotter-pooch** – a person who dribbles a lot
**slouger** – a big thump

**slummick** – to move slowly
**smitch** – smoke
**smitsmats** – little by little
**snarly-barly or snarly grog** – a beetle
**snarly-gig or snarly-horn** – a snail
**snicket** – a very small piece
**snicketty** – very small
**snob** – a cobbler
**soaker** – drunkard
**sodgers** – smoked salt herrings
**sose** – good friends
**spaich-mouth** – conversation
**spare** – very slow
**sparticles** – spectacles
**spicketty** – spotty
**spider-blind** – to whitewash a ceiling
**spilsky** – lean
**splatt** – a small field near a farmhouse
**spreety** – ghostly
**sproil/stroil** – strength
**spuddle** – to stir things up
**spuddlee** – to keep very busy, like me!
**spuddler** – a deliberately awkward person
**squab** – young pigeon
**squayle** – squeal
**stag** – a cock-bird
**stainted** – short-winded
**steeved** – frozen or numbed
**stewer** – dust/fuss
**stid** – to scheme
**stirredge** – a commotion
**stivery** – disordered
**stodger** – a large satisfying bun
**stomickable** – agreeable to the taste
**stooed** – stewed
**strambang** – to fling in a violent fashion
**stubberds** – delicious apples
**stugged** – stuck in a mire or soft ground
**stuggy** – stocky
**stunpile** – a silly fellow
**suent/suant** – even, smooth
**suff** – to sob
**swale** – to burn furze
**swant** – proper
**swarze** – rows
**swill** – to drink heavily
**swimmy** – giddy
**swinkle** – to rinse through or shake out

# T

**tack-hands** – applaud
**tackle** – to beat, to punish
**tacky-lacky** – person at beck and call

**taffety** – dainty
**tallet** – loft above a barn, room next to the roof
**tanchase** – a long run
**tang** – to tie
**tannabye** – definitely
**Tantarabobus** – Satan
**tawd** – toad
**tay** – tea
**teal the tetties** – peel the potatoes
**teddies** – potatoes
**teddy-fat weather** – humid weather
**'telephone English'** – speaking slowly and deliberately whilst trying to conceal one's rich accent
**tell** – chat
**tendersome** – easy-going, mild-mannered
**tervee** – to struggle
**tethers** – buttocks!
**tetties or tiddies** – more potatoes (please)
**thick** – friendly with
**thickee** – that one
**thickety-milk** – boiled milk, with flour and sugar
**thought** – to whittle
**thorting** – ploughing crosswise
**thraipin'** – sorting things out
**thurdle** – miserable
**thurdle gutted** – emaciated or thin
**thust** – thirst
**tiddivate** – to bedeck
**tiggrivate** – to tidy or smarten up
**tilty** – easily offended
**timerson** – nervous disposition
**tishums!** – a burst of sneezing
**titchin'** – touching
**tizzick** – ill with a chest cold
**Topsham pilot** – a cormorant
**toss-pot** – drunkard
**tosticated** – drunk
**tottling** – decrepit
**totty** – of bad character or dizzy
**towse** – busy
**towser** – a hard-working lady
**traipsin** – walking slowly
**trapes** – an untidy woman or slut
**traps** – household goods
**traw** – a trough
**trig** – smart
**trinkrums** – jewellery, silver articles
**trounch** – to walk through a mire
**tucker** – food
**tuck-in** – a hearty meal
**turmits** – turnips

**turveyor** – a shovel for cutting peat
**twaddin** – it wasn't
**tweeny-maid** – a maidservant
**twidden** – it would not
**twily** – meddlesome or troublesome
**twink** – to beat or chastise
**twinkleth** – shakes quickly
**twinkling** – vibrating
**twit** – to perspire
**twittings** – a back lane
**two-eyed steak** – a bloater
**tye** – a rope
**tye-pit** – a well where the water is drawn in a bucket attached to a rope
**tyne** – to extinguish, to tie, to close

# U

**ulker** – big, heavy
**ulking-gert** – very big
**umbessy** – et cetera
**ummits** – large pieces
**umps-ouze** – almshouse
**umsever** – whomsoever
**unbethowted** – remembered
**unket** – lonesome, dismal
**unkid** – weird, bizarre, remote or strange
**unray** – to disrobe or undress
**up-along** – towards home, up-hill
**uppinstock** – mounting-block
**upright-an'-downstraight** – fair and above board
**upsetting** – a christening
**upstore** – an uproar
**upzides with** – revenged upon
**urchin** – a hedgehog
**urn** – run (an anagram!)
**urzells** – ourselves
**uz** – us
**uz be or uz is** – we are
**uz ev** – we have
**uz'l** – we will

# V

**vady** – tainted
**vag** – to trail on the ground
**vagabone** – a tramp
**Vaggus Jack** – a highwayman, a bogie
**vairy** – a weasel
**valiant** – aggressive
**valled-vore** – fell forwards
**valled-vore-skat** – fell flat on face
**vamp** – to sprinkle with water; the font; to increase in knitting
**vamp-dish or church vamp** – the font

**vang** – stick close to, to say
**vang-to** – to act as sponsor, or 'gossip'
**varmer** – farmer
**varry** – to give birth to
**varmints** – vermin
**vast** – fast
**vatty** – filthy
**vauch** – to move quickly
**vawks** – folks
**veak** – to fret
**vear** – piglets
**veesh** – fish
**verrits or vurrits** – ferrets
**vew** – few
**vexed** – upset or angry
**viddy or vittee** – correct
**vilip** – a violet
**Vill-ditch** – February
**vinnied** – bad tempered
**vire-hot** – spanking new
**vish-chowder** – fish seller
**vittles** – food
**voot** – foot
**vore** – front or towards the front
**voredoor** – front door
**vorenoons** – elevenses
**vore-token/voretokeny** – a warning
**vourty** – forty
**voz-bush** – gorse bush
**vulty** – filthy
**vurrid** – forehead
**vurriner** – anyone from outside the district
**vust** – first
**vutty** – dirty
**vuzz** – gorse or furze
**vuzzigant** – house-proud
**vuzz-poll** – having untidy hair

# W

**wab** – tongue
**wacker** – a strong blow
**wacking-gert** – extremely big
**wallage** – an untidy bundle
**wallflowers** – idle folk who hang around street corners
**walsh** – feeble or weak
**wambliness** – an uneasy feeling in the stomach
**wangary** – limp, weary
**want** – a mole
**wantcatcher** – a mole catcher
**want-knap** – mole hill
**want-snap** – a device for catching moles
**wap-eyed** – sleepy
**wapsy** – a wasp, cross, bad-tempered

**warriors** – wallflowers
**wash-a-mouth** – a person who regularly uses foul language
**water-dog** – an otter
**watter-swate** – clean
**waxing-curls** – swollen glands of neck
**waysgoose** – a day out or short break, originally for the print trade
**way-wise** – experienced. worldly
**wee-wow** – squinting/puckered/cross-wise
**Welsh parrot** – a puffin
**weskit** – waistcoat
**western nanny** – a short, sharp shower powered by the prevailing westerly wind
**wether** – castrated sheep
**whate** – wheat
**whatje-come** – what's-his-name
**whift** – to fish from a boat using a hand line
**whips-while** – now and again
**Whipshire** – Tiverton, where, apparently, it was common to whip minor felons rather than sentence them to jail
**whist/wisht** – weird, uncanny, lonely, 'overlooked'; bewitched as in the hounds of the Devil, the Wisht Hounds
**whisterclister/whisterpoop** – a back-handed slap
**Whitstone Hills** – somewhat perversely, the Blackdown Hills – whetstones were quarried at Blackborough in these hills until 1932
**whit-yeth** – white heather
**whoam** – home
**whoop** – a bullfinch
**winnicking** – inferior
**wiss or wuss** – worse
**wisser** – more wise, except in spelling!
**wob** – a lump
**wod** – a small wisp of hay
**wolpy** – turning sour
**wondersome** – wonderful
**wopper-eyed** – tearful
**wordify** – to put into words
**word-of-a-sart** – a dispute
**worrit** – worry
**worts** – whortleberries
**wrangy** – incorrect
**wraxling** – wrestling
**wurdle** – world
**wustest** – without doubt the worst of the worst!

# Y

**yaffers** – heifers
**yaffle or yafful** – a handful

**yammets** – ants
**yamming** – talking with impetus/enthusiasm
**yang** – to mock or deride
**yanzide** – the far side
**Yardie or Yardy** – a term often given to a worker at Devonport Dockyard
**yark** – sprightly or lively
**yarker** – a quick-thinking animal
**yar-yar** – a bumpkin
**yaw-cat** – a feline friend
**yaw** – to bite
**yaws** – ewes
**yeffel** – a heath-like field
**yer** – here, in this place
**yer** – hear
**yer-drops** – earrings
**yett** – hot or heat
**yonsay** – bawling out
**yucks** – hiccoughs (pardon!)
**yu'm** – you are
**yuzzen** – a dung pile or heap

# Z

**Zatterdy** – Saturday
**zamzawed** – sodden, also stewed tea
**zackly** – exactly
**zand** – sand
**zartin** – certain
**zawk** – a silly person
**zaxon** – a sexton
**zex** – six
**Zinday or Zunday** – Sunday
**zober-zides** – a seriously-minded person
**zogging** – dozing
**zoop** – to take long sips
**zour zab** – bad-tempered person
**zuent** – smooth
**zugs** – bogs or mires
**zummat** – something
**zummer** – summer
**zweemy** – dizzy